First published in 2008 by Wayland

Wayland is a division of Hachette Children's Books.

Copyright © Wayland 2008

This paperback edition published in 2012 by Wayland.

Wayland
338 Euston Road
London NW1 3BH

Wayland Australia
Hachette Children's Books
Level 17/207 Kent Street
Sydney, NSW 2000

Managing Editor: Rasha Elsaeed
Editor: Katie Dicker
Picture researcher: Shelley Noronha
Designer: Alix Wood. Illustrator: Catherine Ward
Author dedication: 'For the staff and pupils of
Field Lane Primary School, Rastrick'

Picture Credits
Front cover, bottom right: © Tibor Bognár/CORBIS. Page 6, Figure A: F.Hasler, M.Jentoft-Nilsen, H.Pierce, K.Palaniappan and M.Manyin/NASA. Page 6, Figure B: NASA. Page 7, Figure C: © Crown Copyright 2008, the Met Office. Page 22, Figure A: © Tibor Bognár/CORBIS. Page 22, Figure B: © Frans Lemmens/zefa/Corbis. Page 26, Figure A: P&O Cruises.

Note to parents and teachers: Every effort has been made by the publishers to ensure that websites referred to in the book are suitable for children. However, because of the nature of the Internet, it is impossible to guarantee that the contents of these sites will not be altered. We strongly advise that Internet access is supervised by a responsible adult.

British Library Cataloguing in Publication Data
Gillett, Jack
  Understanding world maps. – (Maps and mapping skills)
  1. Map reading – Juvenile literature 2. World maps –
  Juvenile literature
  I. Title II. Gillett, Meg
  912'.014

ISBN 978 0 7502 6968 1

Printed in China

Wayland is a division of Hachette Children's Books, an Hachette UK Company
www.hachette.co.uk

Understanding
WORLD MAPS

Jack and Meg Gillett

WAYLAND

Contents

Introducing atlases

What is an atlas, and where does its name come from? An atlas is a special type of book. It has a contents page, some chapters and an index. But, unlike a normal book, the chapters of an atlas are a series of maps.

◄ *Atlas carried the weight of the world on his shoulders.*

The word 'atlas' comes from a story told by the Ancient Greeks. In the story, Atlas was a giant who had to carry the world on his shoulders. For this reason, any book that has a set of maps of the world is now called an atlas.

Atlases come in many different forms. Atlases produced in the UK, for example, usually put a map of the British Isles at the front, and place the UK in a central position on any world maps (Figure A).

These maps might change if they are produced in another **country** (Figure B).

The **features** shown on an atlas map are listed in alphabetical order in the index. These might be natural features (such as seas, mountains or weather patterns), or human features (such as population, income or the political rule of different countries). Figure C shows the type of information given in an atlas index.

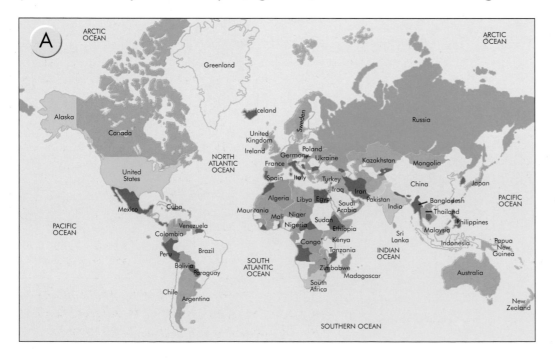

◄ *This map shows the countries of the world from a typical atlas produced in the UK. The countries are different colours to make each one easy to recognise.*

This map shows natural landscape features in a typical atlas produced in Australia. ▶

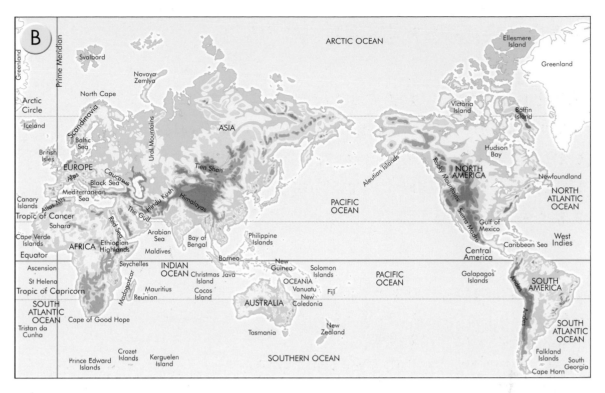

Do it yourself

1. Look inside an atlas produced in the UK and re-arrange these regions to show their order on the contents page: Antarctica, Africa, Asia, Europe, Oceania (shown in some atlases as Australasia), North America, South America, the whole world.

2. Make a list of the type of features shown on maps like the one in Figure A. Make a second list for the type of 'natural' features shown in maps like the one in Figure B.

3. Write the names of the first and last place names in your atlas index. Then add any information about them that is given in the index.

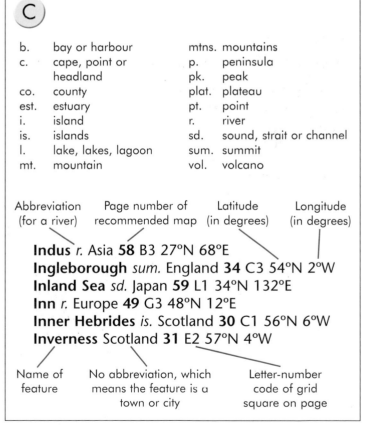

b.	bay or harbour	mtns.	mountains
c.	cape, point or headland	p.	peninsula
		pk.	peak
co.	county	plat.	plateau
est.	estuary	pt.	point
i.	island	r.	river
is.	islands	sd.	sound, strait or channel
l.	lake, lakes, lagoon	sum.	summit
mt.	mountain	vol.	volcano

Abbreviation (for a river)   Page number of recommended map   Latitude (in degrees)   Longitude (in degrees)

Indus *r.* Asia **58** B3 27°N 68°E
Ingleborough *sum.* England **34** C3 54°N 2°W
Inland Sea *sd.* Japan **59** L1 34°N 132°E
Inn *r.* Europe **49** G3 48°N 12°E
Inner Hebrides *is.* Scotland **30** C1 56°N 6°W
Inverness Scotland **31** E2 57°N 4°W

Name of feature   No abbreviation, which means the feature is a town or city   Letter-number code of grid square on page

▲ *This extract shows part of a typical atlas index. You can use an index to identify different features and find out on which map they are located.*

Gathering data

Map-making has been transformed by the use of computers and **satellites**. Satellites gather information about the Earth's surface in a process known as **remote sensing**. This information is transmitted back to Earth, and can be used to produce very accurate maps.

Visible images

Cartographers (map-makers) use three main types of remote-sensed information – visible images, infrared images and radar images. Visible images look like photos taken from space. Satellites are used to record sunlight reflected from land, sea and clouds. These visible images can only be taken during daylight hours.

Infrared images

Infrared images record 'invisible' light produced by land, sea and clouds. The warmer a surface is, the more infrared light it produces. Computers process this information to create images – using pale

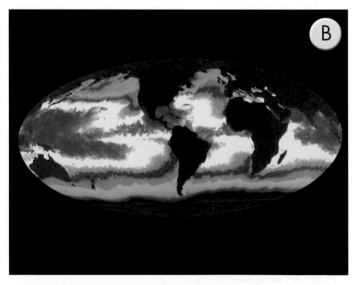

▲ *This visible satellite image shows North and South America and the vast Pacific Ocean. You can also see the 'swirl' of a hurricane (top right).*

▲ *This infrared image shows the Earth's sea surface temperatures. Red areas are the warmest and blue areas are the coldest.*

This radar image shows rainfall over the British Isles. The heaviest rainfall is seen over Wales and northern England. ▶

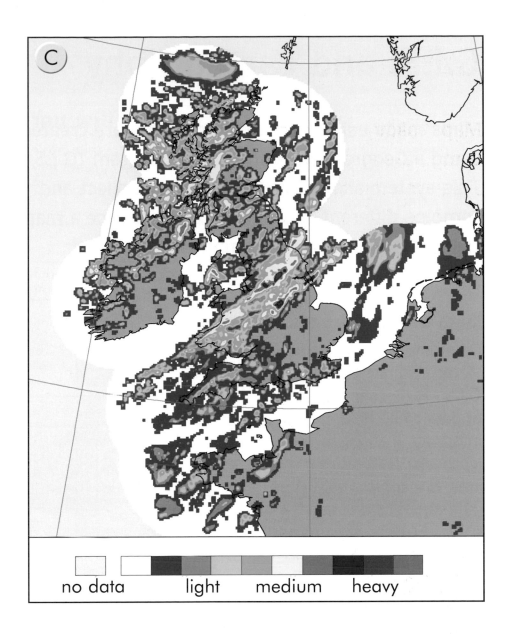

no data   light   medium   heavy

colours to show cool surfaces and dark colours to show warm surfaces. These images can be created at night as well as during the day. Infrared images are often used to record the loss of tropical rainforests in areas such as the Amazon, because they are particularly good at showing vegetation cover.

Radar images

Radar images are created when radio waves are reflected from an object. Like infrared imagery, radar can be used at night as well as during the day. Radar is used by meteorologists to track the movement of rainfall.

Do it yourself

1. Visit the following websites to build up a collection of different images produced by remote sensing:
http://www.metoffice.gov.uk/satpics/latest_VIS.html
http://www.sat.dundee.ac.uk/
(You will have to register first, but it is free and easy to do this)

2. Divide your collection into three categories, one for each of the three types of remote sensing.

Do it yourself

Have a go at making a set of 'layered' data maps of your own, just like a G.I.S.. Follow the instructions in this flow diagram.

Make four tracings of the outline map of Australia (B) – preferably on acetate sheets.

Make a tracing of the relief map of Australia (C) on your first acetate sheet – colouring in the heights of the land, naming the features and adding a key.

On your second blank tracing, draw all of Australia's state boundaries and mark the major cities with a dot. You will need to use an atlas to do this. Name each state and city.

Using your atlas again together with your third acetate sheet, draw a thematic map to show the climate, the ecosystems or possibly the population distribution of Australia. Your choice of map will depend upon those available in your atlas.

Fasten your maps together with a treasury tag, so that they can move freely.

Now, make a hole in the top, left-hand corner of all your maps. Arrange them with the first map you drew at the bottom, and the others on top.

Make a fourth map by choosing another thematic map of Australia to draw onto your last acetate sheet. Again, your choice of map will depend upon your atlas.

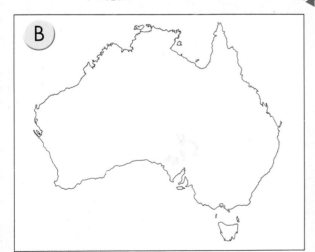

▲ An outline map of Australia.

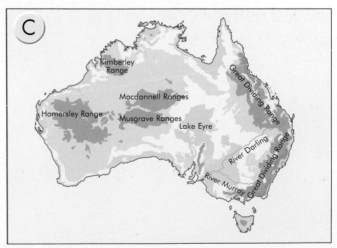

▲ A relief map of Australia.

Well done! You now have a set of layered data maps of Australia. You can use these maps to look for patterns that are linked in some way by comparing different pairs of maps, such as relief (physical) features, climate and population distribution.

Map projections

When cartographers draw world maps, they have to be able to draw the curved surface of the Earth on a flat piece of paper. To do this, the Earth's skin has to be 'peeled off' and then flattened. It's a bit like peeling an orange, then trying to make its skin lie flat.

Figure A shows one way to flatten a map. You can see that the result is not very useful, because the map cuts the land and sea areas into slices and separates them.

Cartographers have three different ways of turning our 3-D Earth into 2-D maps. We call these **map projections** (Figure B).

However, in each projection, some parts of the world have to be stretched out or squashed together.

Cylindrical projections (1) show an image of the globe's surface on a cylinder just touching the **Equator**. The cylinder is then sliced open and unrolled to produce a map. Places close to the Equator are shown very accurately, but those nearer to the Poles are stretched out.

Azimuthal projections (2) are made by projecting the image of one **hemisphere** onto a flat surface, which touches the globe at just one point. The map is accurate where the globe touches the paper, but very distorted at the edges.

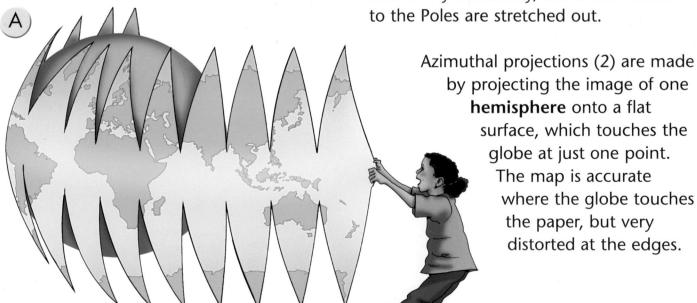

▲ *This is one way of 'flattening' the Earth's curved surface.*

Conical projections (3) are only used to map small areas. The globe's image is projected onto a cone of paper resting on the top of it. The cone is then sliced open, and flattened out. The map is accurate where the globe touches the cone, but the distortion is so great at the cone's point that this is usually cut off!

Do it yourself

1 On an enlarged drawing of the maps in Figure B, use dark shading to show which areas of each map are most distorted. Then use lighter shading to show which areas are most accurate.

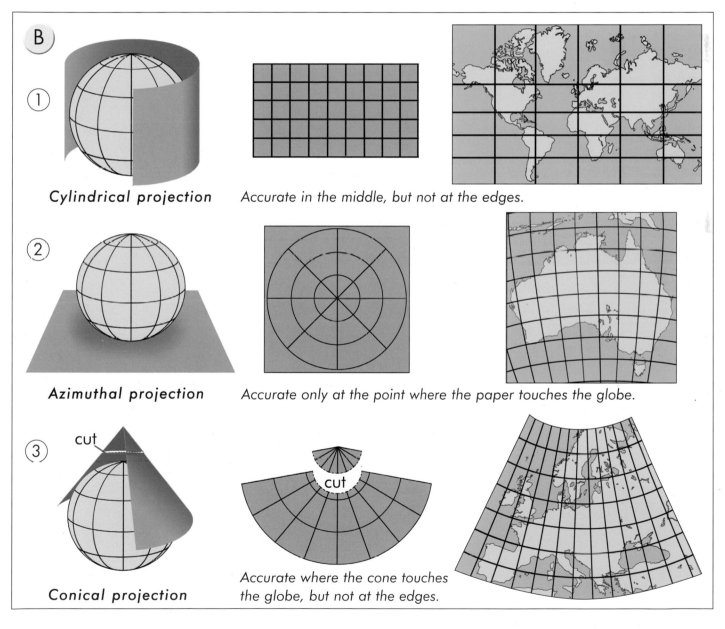

B

① **Cylindrical projection**   *Accurate in the middle, but not at the edges.*

② **Azimuthal projection**   *Accurate only at the point where the paper touches the globe.*

③ cut   cut

Conical projection   *Accurate where the cone touches the globe, but not at the edges.*

▲ Map projections turn our 3-D Earth into a 2-D drawing in a variety of different ways.

Latitude and longitude

Atlas maps use a **latitude** and **longitude** grid system to find the locations of places. Figure A shows how latitude lines are measured in degrees from the Equator and how longitude lines are measured from the **Prime Meridian**, which passes through London.

Figure B shows how we can use latitude and longitude lines to find places on a world map. Latitudes in the Northern Hemisphere have the letter N after them, while those in the Southern Hemisphere have the letter S.

Five lines of latitude have been given names because they are so important. On either side of the Equator are the 'Tropics'. These two lines are special because the Sun passes directly over the places between them twice during the year. The two 'Circles' are also special – the places inside them have 24 hours of darkness in mid-winter, and they have 24 hours of daylight in mid-summer.

▼ *Latitude and longitude lines divide the Earth's surface into sections. These lines are measured in degrees.*

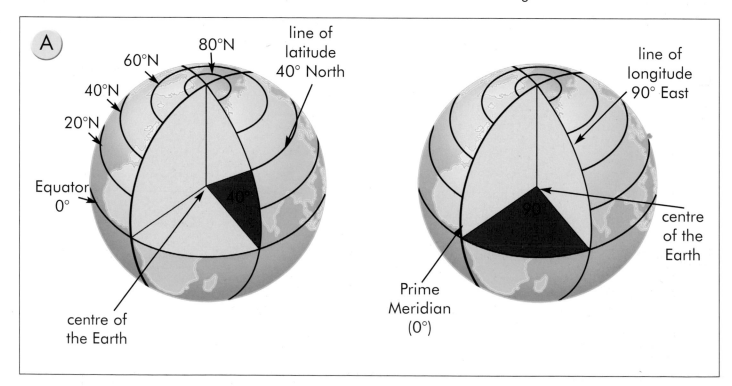

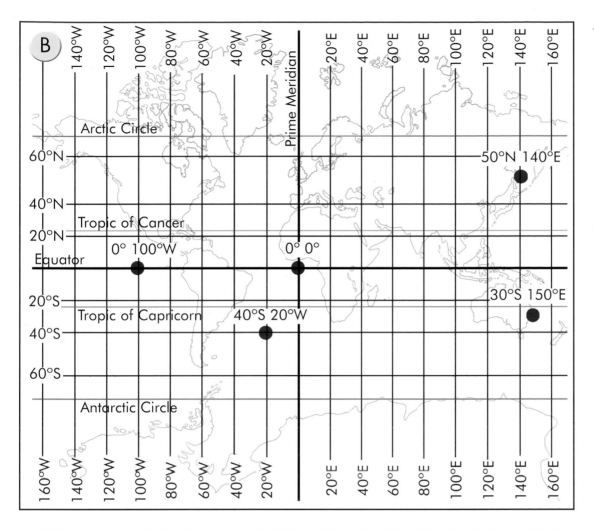

How to find places using lines of latitude and longitude (as shown on the map by the red dots).

Do it yourself

1 **a** Look in an atlas and name the lines of latitude that have the following numbers of degrees:
0°, 23°N, 23°S, 66°N, 66°S.

 b Why do you think that latitude 0° doesn't have a letter?

 c What are the highest numbers of latitude and longitude degrees?

2 Name the continent or ocean at each of these locations:

 a 0° 20°E

 b 0° 160°W

 c 20°S 60°W

 d 30°S 80°E

3 Use your atlas's index to find out which city in each group of three has the smallest latitude (and is therefore nearest to the Equator):

 a Berlin, London, Rotterdam

 b Chicago, Los Angeles, New York

 c Cairo, Cape Town, Rio de Janeiro

 d Jakarta, Nairobi, Singapore

4 Use an atlas map of the Mediterranean Sea to name the islands at:

 a 35°N 25°E

 b 40°N 8°E

 c 35°N 33°E

 d 38°N 13°E

Physical maps

All atlases have physical maps that show the natural features of the Earth's surface, such as landmasses (the **continents**) and oceans. These maps also show the height and shape of the land, the depth of the oceans and features such as deserts and forests (see Figure A).

Maps that show the height and shape of the land can also be called **relief maps**. They give the positions and names of major mountain ranges, the highest mountains, the largest deserts and lakes, and also the longest rivers.

Relief maps are a type of **choropleth map**. Traditionally, mountains and hills are shown on these maps in shades of brown, with yellows and greens being used for lowland. However, if the land is very high, purple and white may also be used for mountain peaks. Blue is used for water features; the lighter blue shades show lakes and shallow seas, whilst darker blue shades mark deep ocean trenches. Most physical maps show only two 'human' features: place names and a grid of latitude and longitude lines.

Do it yourself

1. Use the map on page 15 (and an atlas) to identify the following most outstanding physical features in Africa, Asia, Europe, North America, South America and Oceania:

   a Highest mountain
   b Largest desert (not Europe or North America)
   c Largest lake
   d Longest river

2. Which of your answers is the world's most outstanding feature of its kind?

3. Use the Internet to discover the surface area of each of the world's oceans, then list them in size order – starting with the largest.

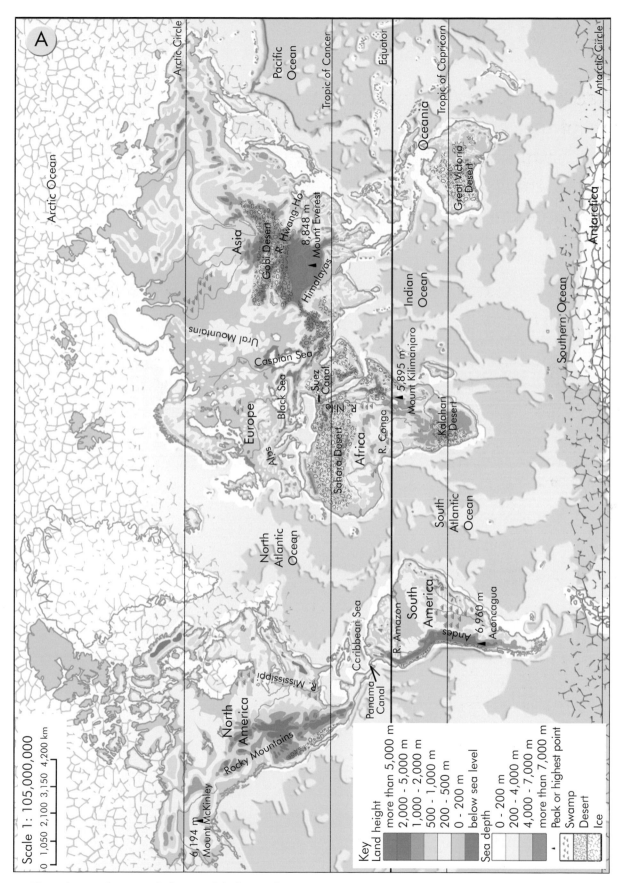

A

Scale 1: 105,000,000

0 1,050 2,100 3,150 4,200 km

Key

Land height
more than 5,000 m
2,000 – 5,000 m
1,000 – 2,000 m
500 – 1,000 m
200 – 500 m
0 – 200 m
below sea level

Sea depth
0 – 200 m
200 – 4,000 m
4,000 – 7,000 m
more than 7,000 m
Peak or highest point
Swamp
Desert
Ice

Arctic Circle

Arctic Ocean

Pacific Ocean

Tropic of Cancer

Equator

Tropic of Capricorn

Antarctic Circle

Asia

Gobi Desert

R. Hwang-Ho

8,848 m
Mount Everest

Himalayas

Ural Mountains

Caspian Sea

Black Sea

Suez Canal

Europe

Alps

Sahara Desert

Africa

R. Congo

5,895 m
Mount Kilimanjaro

Indian Ocean

Kalahari Desert

Oceania

Great Victoria Desert

Southern Ocean

Antarctica

North Atlantic Ocean

South Atlantic Ocean

Caribbean Sea

Panama Canal

R. Mississippi

North America

Rocky Mountains

6,194 m
Mount McKinley

R. Amazon

South America

Andes

6,960 m
Aconcagua

▲ This physical map of the world shows features such as continents, mountains, oceans and deserts.

15

Map patterns

Many people think that information shown on maps is easier to understand than facts given in numbers and words! This is because maps are 'pictures'. They help us to visualise information – and our memories are good at remembering picture images.

Maps help us to answer questions by showing 'picture patterns', like those in Figure A. We can see that the highest mountains are in the middle of the Lake District; also that the lakes are long and narrow, pointing outwards from the middle, like spokes on a wheel. By studying these two patterns, scientists have worked out how they are linked. During the **Ice Age**, **glaciers** moved down from the central mountains and their hard ice produced long, narrow, deep valleys. These valleys were later flooded to form the lakes.

Maps also help us to identify and understand worldwide patterns. Figure B gives us three global 'picture-patterns', for example. It shows the locations of major **earthquakes**, active **volcanoes** and **plate margins** – the boundaries of large sections of the Earth's crust. All three patterns are closely linked. Look at the 'Do it yourself' box to find out how! Scientists look at the places where earthquakes or volcanoes have occurred and try to predict where and when other natural disasters might happen.

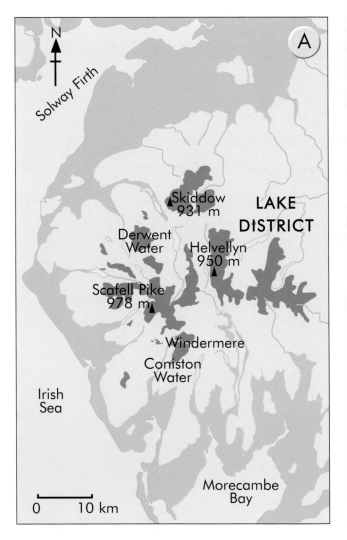

▲ *A physical map of the Lake District showing water features and high land.*

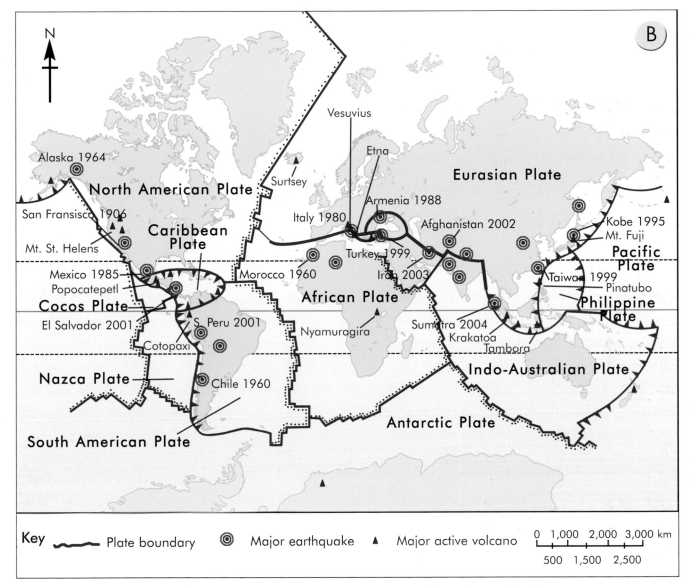

▲ *This map shows the locations of the Earth's plate margins, earthquakes and volcanoes.*

Do it yourself

1 Answer the following questions about Figure B:

  a Does there seem to be a pattern to the way the earthquakes are located? Why do you think this is?

  b Is there a similar pattern to the distribution of the volcanoes? Why do you think this is?

  c Are these two patterns in similar places? Why do you think this is?

2 Look at these Internet sites to help you to explain more fully how – and why – all three patterns are linked:

http://www.geography.learnontheinternet. co.uk/topics/structureofearth.html

http://www.extremescience.com/ PlateTectonicsmap.htm

Climate maps and graphs

Climate is a term used to describe the kind of weather that places usually experience over a long period of time. Some countries are hot and have long, dry summers while other countries are cold or have a lot of rain. The map in Figure B shows five different types of climate.

Climate maps are examples of **thematic maps**. The climate map in Figure B shows that the hottest climates occur near to the Equator, and that the coldest ones are nearest to the Poles. These patterns suggest that climate type is closely linked to latitude. However, along the line of the Equator, you will see that some places have a cooler, temperate climate. This is because, wherever you are in the world, temperatures drop as you climb high mountains – and several places along the Equator are very high!

Similarly, the climate in the Himalayas is 'Polar', because this mountain range is so high that temperatures are always below freezing and the landscape is one of permanent snow and ice.

Figure A is also a thematic map, but shows lines called **isopleths**. This map gives information about average temperatures across Europe. Isopleths like these have a special name. Because they join places with equal temperature (and temperatures are measured on a thermometer), they are called isotherms.

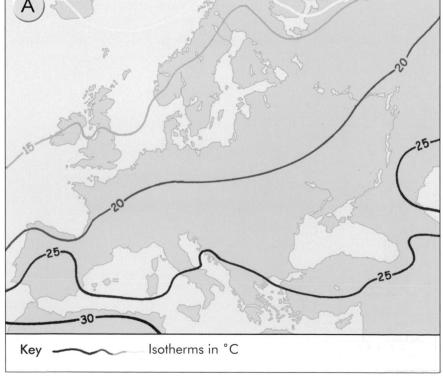

Key — Isotherms in °C

This isopleth map shows average temperatures across Europe in the summer.

Do it yourself

1 Use the map on page 15 to name the mountain in East Africa and the mountain range in South America which both lie on the Equator.

2 Use the five graphs in Figure B to help you to complete a copy of this table:

Type of climate	Highest temperature	Lowest temperature	Amount of rainfall in the wettest month	Amount of rainfall in the driest month
Cold (Russia)				
Dry (Australia)				
Polar (Canada)				
Temperate (France)				
Tropical (Brazil)				

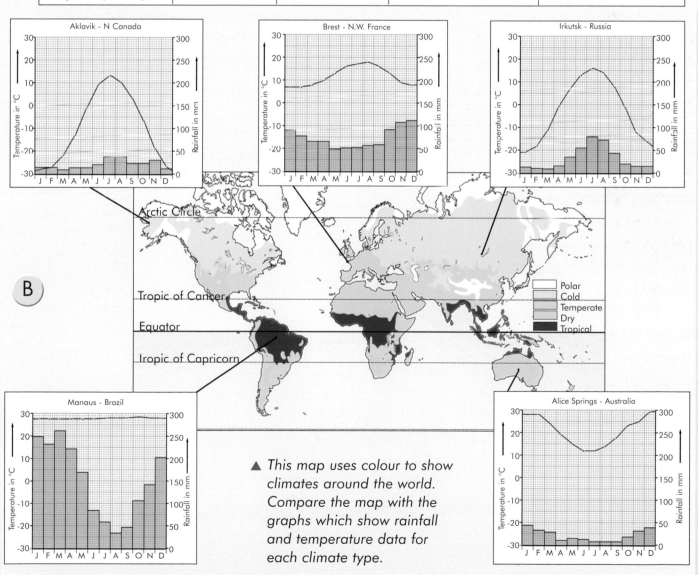

B

▲ This map uses colour to show climates around the world. Compare the map with the graphs which show rainfall and temperature data for each climate type.

Countries

Some atlas maps show information that is not about the natural world at all. These maps are used to show human features such as place names, railways and cities. They can also show details about individual countries – where their borders are and which other places they govern.

Most of the countries of the world have existed for a very long time, but their names do not always stay the same! Sometimes, countries have disappeared – like Czechoslovakia which became the Czech Republic and Slovakia.

Every country, however big or small, protects the **borders** that separate it from its neighbours. But not all countries agree where their international borders should lie (Figure B). For example, India and Pakistan have long disputed their right to Kashmir.

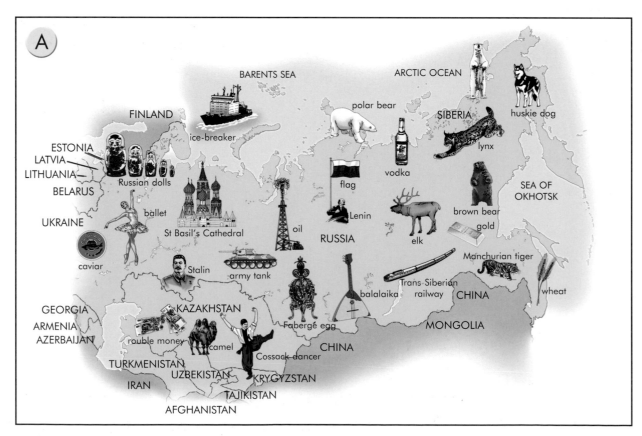

A

BARENTS SEA · ARCTIC OCEAN · polar bear · SIBERIA · huskie dog · FINLAND · ice-breaker · lynx · ESTONIA · LATVIA · LITHUANIA · vodka · BELARUS · Russian dolls · flag · SEA OF OKHOTSK · UKRAINE · ballet · Lenin · brown bear · St Basil's Cathedral · oil · RUSSIA · gold · elk · caviar · Stalin · army tank · Manchurian tiger · Trans-Siberian railway · balalaika · CHINA · wheat · GEORGIA · KAZAKHSTAN · Fabergé egg · MONGOLIA · ARMENIA · AZERBAIJAN · rouble money · camel · CHINA · TURKMENISTAN · Cossack dancer · UZBEKISTAN · KRYGYZSTAN · IRAN · TAJIKISTAN · AFGHANISTAN

▲ This map shows some of the things that Russia is famous for.
What drawings would be shown on a map of your country?

Do it yourself

1 What natural features act as borders between these pairs of countries?:
  a England and France
  b France and Spain
  c Bulgaria and Romania
  d Tanzania and Uganda

2 On a copy of a map showing any country (except Russia):
  a write the names of any neighbouring countries, seas or oceans outside its borders.
  b using Figure A as an example, draw some well-known symbols of your chosen country.

Atlas maps shade neighbouring countries in different colours to make each one easy to recognise. These same colours are used to identify the ownership of any nearby islands (Figure C). Rivers, lakes, mountain ranges and latitude lines can act as international borders.

Key

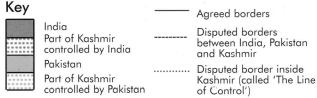

▩ India	—— Agreed borders
⦂⦂ Part of Kashmir controlled by India	------- Disputed borders between India, Pakistan and Kashmir
▨ Pakistan	·········· Disputed border inside Kashmir (called 'The Line of Control')
⦂⦂ Part of Kashmir controlled by Pakistan	

▲ For many years, India and Pakistan have not been able to agree which country should rightfully own Kashmir.

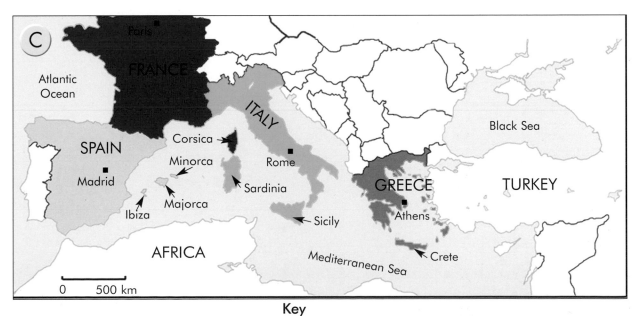

▲ Different colours show which countries these Mediterranean Sea islands belong to.

Key

■ French territory	■ Italian territory	〜 Country border
■ Greek territory	■ Spanish territory	▪ Capital city

21

Populations

Nearly half of all the people in the world live in **urban areas** such as towns and cities. Many of the largest urban areas are on the coast, where the land is flatter. Some of these urban areas are the capital cities of their countries.

Here are three statements about cities that are completely untrue!

- All capital cities are the biggest cities in their countries. Wrong! Washington DC is the capital of the USA, but has only a seventh of New York City's population.

- Only very rich people live in **'millionaire cities'**. Wrong! Millionaire cities simply have over 1,000,000 inhabitants!

- **Densely-populated areas** such as cities are inhabited only by people who are not very intelligent. Wrong! Densely-populated areas have lots of people living quite close together (Figure A) and it doesn't matter how intelligent they are! Such regions are the opposite of **sparsely-populated areas** (Figure B).

▲ Cities like Cairo are very densely-populated areas.

▲ The Sahara Desert, in North Africa, is one of the world's most sparsely-populated regions.

Figure C shows some of the ways that atlas maps can show information about cities, and which parts of a country are densely- or sparsely-populated.

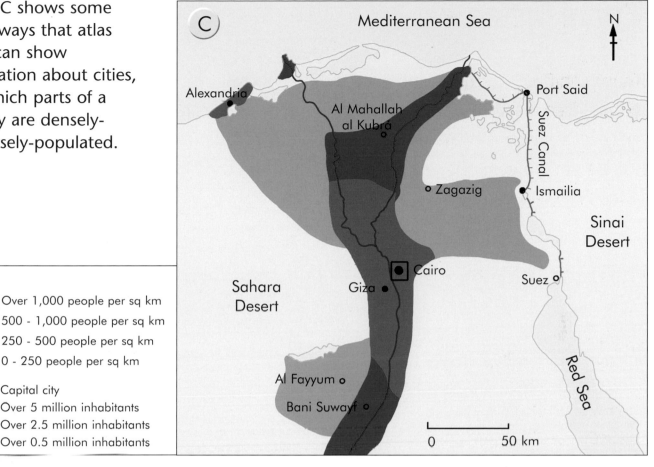

▲ *This map shows population density in Egypt.*

Do it yourself

1 How does your atlas show:
    a how many people live in a city?
    b whether a city is the capital of its country?
    c whether large areas are densely- or sparsely-populated?

2 Use your atlas to find out which countries these cities are in and whether they are capital cities: Canberra, Dhaka, Delhi, Islamabad, Lagos, Mexico City, Paris, Sao Paulo, Shanghai, Singapore (be careful!) and Toronto.

3 **a** Find the following places on maps of the world showing mountainous areas, hot deserts, ice sheets and tropical rainforests: 0° 60°W; 20°N 50°E; 80°S 120°E; 30°N 90°E; 30°N 13°E.
    b Is each of these places densely- or sparsely-populated?

Time zones

If you wanted to telephone a friend in Australia or Pakistan, would it cross your mind to think what time it might be there? Or even whether it is day or night? Your friend might not be very pleased if you called in the middle of the night!

The Earth's rotation

The times of day and night in any part of the world depend on the time of sunrise and sunset. These times vary because the Earth rotates on its axis – it makes one complete turn before coming back to exactly the same position 24 hours later. Figure A shows this rotation and how it affects the time of day around the world.

Time changes are never-ending – and this can cause big problems. Imagine if you travelled by train and had to constantly alter your watch to keep up with the Earth's rotation! Luckily, these problems are avoided by dividing the Earth into 24 one-hour **time zones** (Figure B). Countries like the UK are in one time zone, but Russia is so vast that it covers eleven!

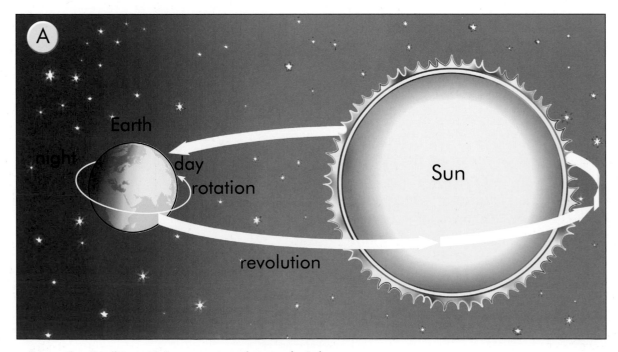

Earth

night   day
         rotation

Sun

revolution

▲ *How the Earth's rotation creates day and night.*

Do it yourself

1 a How many times would you have to change the time on your watch if you were flying from the west coast of Australia to its east coast?

  b Would you put your watch 'forward' or 'back' during this flight?

2 Using Figure B, work out what the local times in Washington DC (USA), Beijing (China) and Sydney (Australia) would be if you were in London and your watch read 2.30 p.m.

3 Use the Internet to find out what 'jet lag' is. How does it affect passengers on very long flights?

The world's 24 time zones. ▶

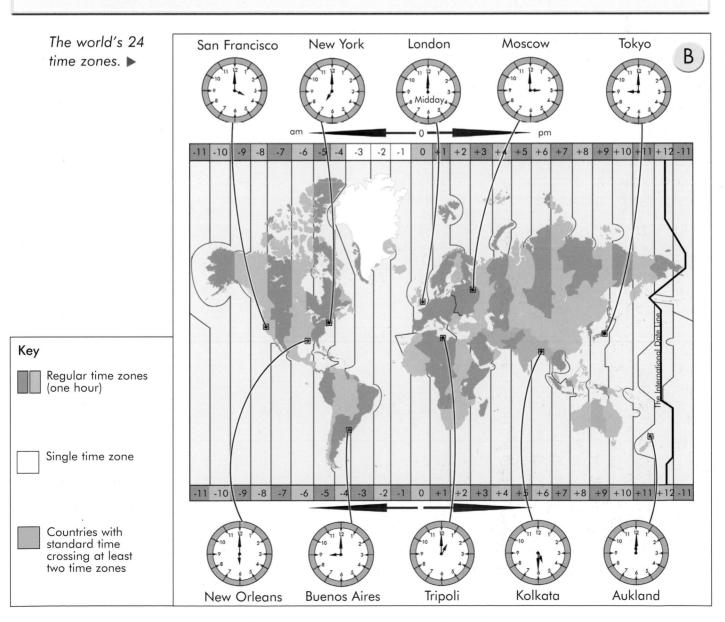

Key

Regular time zones (one hour)

Single time zone

Countries with standard time crossing at least two time zones

Use your skills: Global travel

Every year, about 1.5 million Britons book a holiday on a cruise liner. Between January and March, almost 2,000 passengers sailed on the luxury cruise liner AURORA (Figure A). The table below shows the places the ship visited after leaving England on 7th January.

▲ The 76,000-ton cruise liner AURORA.

B

Date	Place visited	Location of visit	Logo
7th January	Leave Southampton	England	
15th January	Barbados	West Indies	
19th January	Sail through the Panama Canal	Panama, Central America	
26th January	San Francisco	United States of America	
31st January	Honolulu	Hawaii, middle of the Pacific Ocean	
11th February	Auckland	New Zealand	
14th February	Sydney	Australia	
26th February	Hong Kong	China	
2nd March	Bangkok	Thailand	
4th March	Singapore	Singapore	
9th March	Colombo	Sri Lanka	
12th March	Mumbai	India	
19th March	Sail through the Suez Canal	Egypt	
21st March	Athens	Greece	
24th March	Barcelona	Spain	
28th March	Return to Southampton	England	

▲ The itinerary of the AURORA's 80-night cruise.

Do it yourself

1 Use your atlas maps to find all the places visited by the AURORA, then:

   a mark with a dot and name these places in their correct locations on a copy of the map at the back of the book. You can enlarge this map if you wish.

   b join all these places with a single line to show the sea route taken by the ship.

   c colour and name all the countries which the ship visited.

   d use your completed map to work out the dates when the AURORA probably crossed the Equator, the Prime Meridian and the International Date Line.

   e use the scale on the map to estimate the total distance travelled by the ship. Which of these three distances is closest to your estimate?
23,000 km; 48,000 km; 67,000 km.

2 Figure C shows why places on the Earth's surface have their seasons at different times of the year. Use it to explain why the AURORA's passengers chose a cruise that took place during January, February and March.

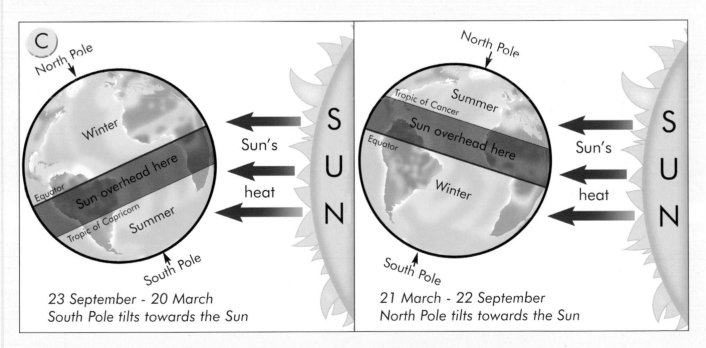

▲ *The four seasons are affected by the position of the Earth in relation to the Sun.*

3 Choose any four places visited by the AURORA (each one in a different continent); then use the Internet to discover the attractions of each place for tourists. Use this information to make a display advertising the cruise to future passengers.

Use your skills: Quiz time

Test out your skills and use an atlas to answer the following questions.

1 Name these islands, which are all in the British Isles. Some of them have been drawn to different scales, but all share the same North direction.

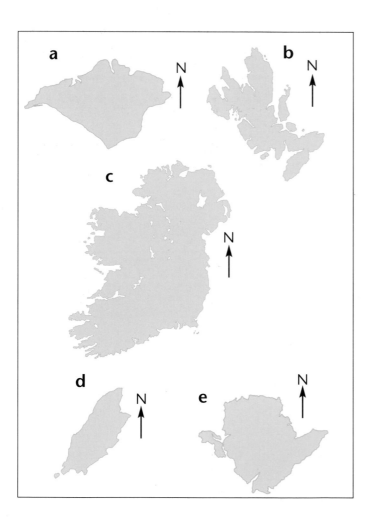

2 Now name these European countries, which have not been drawn with North pointing in the same direction!

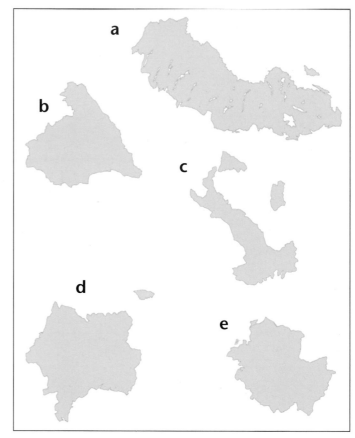

3 Which is the odd one in each of these groups of four places? and why?
   a Andes Everest Himalayas Rockies
     (They are all very high places, but …)
   b Amazon Nile Mississippi Victoria
     (They are all very large water features, but …)
   c England Republic of Ireland Scotland Wales
     (They all countries in the British Isles, but …)

d Antarctica Africa Asia The Arctic
(They are all large global regions, but …)

e Caspian Sea Gobi Desert River Ganges Turkey
(They are all places in Asia, but …).

4 Which is the correct answer in each of these multiple-choice questions?

a The capital city of a country is always:
- a city by the coast.
- its largest city.
- the city where its government is.

b Maps of Australia show that:
- Australia's capital city is Sydney.
- most Australians live on the coast.
- this country's most densely-populated area is in its centre.

c All millionaire cities:
- are at least one million years old.
- are populated by rich people who are millionaires.
- are home to at least one million people.

d Krakatoa was the site of one of the world's worst:
- droughts.
- earthquakes.
- volcanic eruptions.

e World maps drawn using a cylindrical projection have:
- latitude and longitude lines which are both straight.
- latitude and longitude lines which are both curved.
- straight latitude lines, but curved longitude lines.

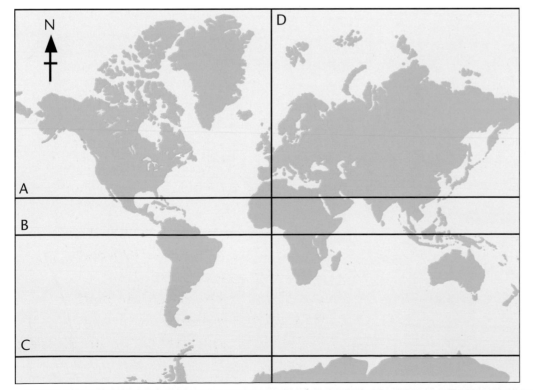

5 Name the four lines of latitude and longitude shown by the letters A – D on this map.

Glossary

Border A boundary line that separates countries that are next to each other.

Choropleth map A map that has colour shading to show a distribution pattern.

Climate The kind of weather which takes place during a typical year.

Continent One of the world's six largest land areas.

Country An area of land that has its own government, identity and national flag.

Densely-populated area A place where many people live close together.

Earthquake A sudden, violent movement of the rocks at or below the Earth's surface.

Equator An imaginary line that runs from west to east around the middle of the Earth.

Feature A part of a landscape, such as a house or a wood.

Geographical Information System (G.I.S.) A computer system for storing 'layers' of different information.

Glacier A large body of ice that flows along the bottom of a valley.

Hemisphere One half of the Earth. The Northern Hemisphere is above the Equator; the Southern Hemisphere is below it.

Ice Age A period of time when temperatures were below 0°C in many parts of the world.

Isopleth A line which links places on a map having the same value.

Latitude line An imaginary line running from east to west around the globe parallel to the Equator.

Longitude line An imaginary line running from north to south around the globe and at right angles to the Equator.

Map projection A way in which the 3-D Earth is changed to a 2-D map surface. The three types of map projection are: azimuthal, conical and cylindrical.

Millionaire city A city that has at least one million people.

Plate margin The edge of a 'plate' – one of the huge parts of the Earth's surface.

Prime Meridian Line of longitude 0° that passes through Greenwich, London.

Relief (physical) map A map that shows the height and shape of the land.

Remote sensing The production of infrared, radar and visible images using satellites.

Satellite A machine that orbits above Earth.

Sparsely-populated area An area in which very few people live.

Thematic map A map that shows just one type of information.

Time zone An area of the world in which every clock is set to the same time.

Urban area An area that has many buildings.

Volcano A mountain made from layers of ash and solid lava from below the Earth's surface.

Index

Answers

p11 Cylindrical projections: most distorted along their northern and southern edges. Azimuthal projections: most distorted along the northern edges. Conical projections: most distorted at the top (where they are cut off) and some distortion along the southern edge.

p13 1a) 0° Equator; 23°N Tropic of Cancer; 23°S Tropic of Capricorn; 66°N Arctic Circle; 66°S Antarctic Circle **1b)** It is the middle, the line from which other lines of latitude are measured. **1c)** Highest latitude 90°; highest longitude 180°. **2a)** Africa **2b)** Pacific Ocean **2c)** South America **2d)** Indian Ocean. **3a)** London **3b)** Los Angeles **3c)** Rio de Janeiro **3d)** Singapore. **4a)** Crete **4b)** Sardinia **4c)** Cyprus **4d)** Sicily.

p14 1) Africa: Highest mountain – Mount Kilimanjaro. Largest desert – Sahara. Largest lake – Victoria. Longest river – Nile. **Asia:** Highest mountain – Mount Everest. Largest desert – Gobi. Largest lake – Baikal. Longest river – Chang Jiang (Yangtze). **Europe:** Highest mountain – Mount Elbrus. Largest lake – Ladoga. Longest river – Volga. **North America:** Highest mountain – Mount McKinley. Largest lake – Superior. Longest river – Mississippi/Missouri. **South America:** Highest mountain – Aconcagua. Largest desert – Atacama. Largest lake – Titicaca. Longest river – Amazon. **Oceania:** Highest mountain – Puncak Jaya (Indonesia). Largest desert – Great Sandy Desert (Australia). Largest lake – Lake Eyre (Australia). Longest river – Murray/Darling (Australia). **2)** Highest mountain: Mount Everest. Largest desert: Sahara. Largest lake: Superior. Longest river: Nile. **3)** Pacific – 155,557 km²; Atlantic – 76,762 km²; Indian – 68,556 km²; Southern – 20,327 km²; Arctic – 14,056 km².

p17 1a) Yes; Earthquakes are generally along or very close to plate margins. **1b)** Yes; Volcanoes are generally close to plate margins. **1c)** Yes; plate margins are the places where the Earth's crust is most active/unstable.

p19 1) East Africa: Mount Kilimanjaro; South America: Andes. **2)** Cold: Highest temp 16°C; Lowest temp -21°C; Wettest month 80 mm; Driest month 10 mm. Dry: Highest temp 29°C; Lowest temp 12°C; Wettest month 45 mm; Driest month 8 mm. Polar: Highest temp 13°C; Lowest temp -28°C; Wettest month 38 mm; Driest month 10 mm. Temperate: Highest temp 18°C; Lowest temp 7°C; Wettest month 110 mm; Driest month 50 mm. Tropical: Highest temp 29°C; Lowest temp 28°C; Wettest month 260 mm; Driest month 35 mm.

p21 1a) Sea (English Channel) **1b)** Mountains (Pyrenees) **1c)** River (Danube) **1d)** Lake (Victoria)

p23 2) Canberra: Australia (capital). Dhaka: Bangladesh (capital). Delhi: India (not capital). Islamabad: Pakistan (capital). Lagos: Nigeria (not capital). Mexico City: Mexico (capital). Paris: France (capital). Sao Paulo: Brazil (not capital). Shanghai: China (not capital). Singapore: Singapore (capital). Toronto: Canada (not capital). **3a)** Tropical rainforest; desert; ice; mountains; desert. **3b)** All are sparsely-populated.

p25 1a) Twice **1b)** Forward **2)** 2:30 pm London, 9:30 am Washington, 10:30 pm Beijing, 12:30 am (next day) Sydney

p27 1e) 48,000 km **2)** It is winter in Europe and the people travelling on Aurora want to escape the poor weather and spend winter in the Southern Hemisphere where it's summer.

p28 1a) Isle of Wight **1b)** Isle of Skye **1c)** Ireland **1d)** Isle of Man **1e)** Anglesey **2a)** Sweden **2b)** Spain **2c)** Italy **2d)** France **2e)** Germany **3a)** Mount Everest because it's a single mountain; the rest are mountain ranges **3b)** Lake Victoria because this is a lake; the others are rivers **3c)** Republic of Ireland because the others are part of the United Kingdom **3d)** The Arctic because this is the only ocean **3e)** Turkey because it is the only country in the list **4a)** the city where its government is. **4b)** most Australians live on the coast. **4c)** are home to at least one million people. **4d)** volcanic eruptions. **4e)** latitude and longitude lines which are both straight. **5)** A: Tropic of Cancer; B: Equator; C: Antarctic Circle; D: Prime Meridian.